LATIN AMERICAN PUBLICATIONS FUND

LATIN AMERICAN PUBLICATIONS FUND
31 TAVISTOCK SQUARE
LONDON, WC1H 9HA

Michael Kuczynski

A Peruvian who worked for eight years in the Research Department of the International Monetary Fund. He now holds the David Joslin Memorial Fellowship at Pembroke College, Cambridge, where he is studying Latin America's links with the international monetary system.

David Huelin

Manager of the Economics Department at Lloyds and Bolsa International Bank Limited, having held that post in the Economic Research Department of BOLSA from 1952. He lived and worked in Argentina from 1936-50 and has paid numerous visits to Latin America, the most recent one to Colombia, Ecuador, Peru and Venezuela late in 1972. He has published extensively on Latin American economic affairs.

Contents

Planned Development in the Andean Group

INDUSTRIAL POLICY AND TRADE LIBERALIZATION

Michael Kuczynski

Introduction

THREE YEARS AFTER the negotiations began, a 'sub-regional integration agreement', now officially known as the Cartagena Agreement, was signed on 26th May 1969 by representatives of Bolivia, Chile, Colombia, Ecuador and Peru. The agreement came into force for these countries five months later on 16th October 1969. Together with its ancillary rulings and subsequent regulations, it is referred to as the Andean Pact. Venezuela, a party to the negotiations, eventually subscribed to the Pact in February 1973. Legally speaking the Pact was negotiated within the ambit of the Latin American Free Trade Association (Lafta) established in 1960 by the Treaty of Montevideo; hence the epithet 'sub-regional' of the title. In practical terms the link with the Lafta is somewhat ambivalent, but still significant.

Two instruments of the Pact pre-date the Cartagena Agreement. The Andean Development Corporation, of which Venezuela has been a member from the start, was created in February 1968 to act as the financial promoter, so to speak, of the Pact's purposes. And in July 1968 a first agreement on petrochemicals was reached between Bolivia, Chile, Colombia and Peru. It is a limited agreement, also negotiated within the Lafta; but in more ways than one it has become expressive of the history of the Andean Pact, its hopes and fears.

The object of the Pact is to establish a common market among the members. The process is to entail *i.* the liberalization of trade within the sub-region; *ii.* the adoption of policies in common, notably for the external tariff and the treatment of foreign capital; and *iii.* certain

1

guarantees that the benefits will be equitably distributed among the members. The bulk of the process is designed to be complete by the early 1980s, with some straggling elements falling into place in the course of that decade. Schedules and deadlines were set in the Cartagena Agreement to ensure that the Pact's authorities clock round the obstacle course fast enough to be on time at the finish. The highest authority, equivalent to the Council of Ministers of the European Communities, is the Commission; and its 'decisions' are the main implementing instruments of the Pact after the Cartagena Agreement itself.

The predominant concern of the Andean Pact is to influence the course of industrial development in the sub-region: what is to be manufactured, where, and with how much competition. Other provisions remain sketchy, but those which constitute 'industrial policy', by far the most numerous, have from the start approached a mechanical degree of precision and consistency. This may seem forceful to some and naive to others, for reasons that will be outlined below. Suffice it to note here that the Pact draws this form from being a particularly deliberate attempt to apply to policy a distillation of the lessons of economic history.

For a decade or more, from 1954 to 1966, one South American country after another ran into trouble with its manufactures; output, in some cases already well-established, wobbled around a weak trend without gathering momentum. Explanations of this arrested development ranged from the adversity of the terms of trade to the neglect of agriculture at home. In the 1960s, when an unprecedented expansion of the world's rich countries had redressed the terms of trade and considerable amounts of money had become available for investment overseas, and still manufacturing lingered in South America, attention shifted to the interpretation which lies at the heart of the Andean Pact (and of the Lafta before it). It runs as follows.

The average country of South America by itself still provides too small a base, in terms of resources and markets, for modern methods of manufacturing. Yet in the 1950s, for reasons lost in the history of the balance of payments (and because the process is self-reinforcing), each country strayed further and further into excessive levels of tariff protection for manufactures. The result was side-by-side inefficiency; there could be no complementation of resources across borders, products proliferated without specialization, scale and location were often quite uneconomic, and funds for reinvestment were generated only at great cost. Protection strengthened its vested interests; other sectors, notably agriculture, suffered; the balance of payments sickened; and industry fared no better for it.

There was of course some foreign investment in these protected markets, and it often did better than local enterprise; world-wide companies can spread some of their fixed costs over operations in several countries. But, like their national counterparts, the foreign companies stopped short at exports: they might not have been profitable; and in any case some companies were bound by market-sharing agreements among subsidiaries in different countries.

All of these difficulties — the interpretation goes on — multiplied at the threshold into heavier 'basic' industries, such as iron and steel, chemicals, paper, machinery, and motor vehicles. The list of such industries became a *leitmotiv* in the design of the Andean Pact.

The prescription of integration follows quite straightforwardly from this interpretation. The opening-up of borders and the adoption of common policies allows new investment to be planned for a larger market. There is a better chance — though of course no certainty — that different stages of assembly will find, or be forcibly directed to, efficient locations; and there is more scope for specialization and complementation. It is essentially autarky on a broader base.

At the same time, however, there are potential disadvantages in integration. In duplicate industries, the country with the weakest may not be able to withstand competition from its neighbours — nor, indeed, is it intended for efficiency that it should do so. New investment may be concentrated, also for very good reasons, where industrialization is already most implanted, so that, in the absence of a compensating mechanism, backward countries might fare better on their own autarkic devices, at least for the time being. Foreign companies, with world-wide connexions, may be the first and chief beneficiaries of the larger market, because of their centralized structure, their access to finance, and their expertise at moving raw materials and parts around to the point of least-cost assembly.

The likelier an integration effort is to yield a suitable base for heavy industrial development (because of the constellation of countries involved, their size, resources, and past history), the greater is the need for guarantees that the benefits will be equitably distributed. Aside from a general will to that effect, such guarantees may take two forms: the common industrial policy may be sufficiently *dirigiste*, through exclusive rights to production, exemptions from free trade, and the like, to ensure that there is something in it for every member; or the losers in the market-place may be compensated by transfers of funds. The latter are notoriously difficult to negotiate.

The constellation of countries in the Lafta was such that each always had at least one other's competition to fear in some product, and a lobby to placate at home. The Treaty of Montevideo scheduled negotiations product by product, and there was no guarantee that after the swings and roundabouts the advantages to each country would even out — the less so as the negotiations trailed further and further into the future. Therefore, bird-in-hand, and clearly against the logic of integration, the negotiators clung to piecemeal reciprocity on every item, and eventually the effort stalled.

It is significant that of the 18 so-called 'complementarity agreements' reached under the Lafta up to the end of 1972, all cover narrow categories of components rather than whole sectors, and none embraces the whole membership of the Lafta. Mostly the agreements were instigated by foreign companies operating on both sides of a border, and interested in free movement across it for their wares. The petrochemical agreement of 1968 between Bolivia, Chile, Colombia and Peru — Lafta No. 6 — is no exception in this respect.

In the Andean Pact, however, both the ground-rules and the constellation of countries show much more promise. The impulse came from Chile and Colombia, whose manufacturing sectors are advanced and, as luck would have it, fairly complementary. In exchange for a more or less automatic transition to a free sub-regional market, they were willing to grant extensive and explicit industrial advantages to the two most backward countries, Bolivia and Ecuador. In an intermediate position, Peru and Venezuela had more to hope and fear for their industries. They obtained agreement that liberalization should be drawn out over a longer period than Chile and Colombia had hoped (11 years instead of 6), though remaining just as automatic. In settling to join, Peru also fastened on the prospect that the forthcoming allocation of new investment would be sufficiently *dirigiste* to give its industry a place in the sun. Venezuela took longer to come to terms with the others; when it did so, at the beginning of 1973, it was roughly on the same terms as Peru but on the opposite understanding, to wit that *dirigisme* would be contained — at least in industries such as petrochemicals, where Venezuela already has an important stake.

As the common market comes into being, will industrial policy be left mostly to the hidden hand of market forces, or will it entail forcible allocation visibly negotiated ? And, if one rather than the other, will it make much difference ? These questions are still open, likely to remain so for the 1970s, and lively ones for this paper — despite the mechanistic precision of the Pact's provisions, and despite the decisions taken so far. It is time to turn to this detail.

The Andean Pact's content in industrial policy can best be discussed under five headings, of which four will be extensively examined below. These four are: *i.* the liberalization of trade within the group; *ii.* the external tariff; *iii.* the exceptional treatment of Bolivia and Ecuador; and *iv.* plans for joint industrial development. The last-mentioned are perhaps closest to conventional notions of 'industrial policy' in a common market; they include the so-called 'sectoral programmes of industrial development' (SPID) which are such a striking feature of the Cartagena Agreement, and which have been compared — optimistically no doubt — to the European Coal and Steel Community. But the elements under the three other headings are likely to be just as significant, if not more so, in determining what is to be manufactured, where, and with how much competition.

The fifth heading concerns various measures of *harmonization* and *cooperation* which are no less important in principle for being miscellaneous in practice. The Cartagena Agreement declares that common policies should be adopted in various fields: monetary, fiscal, exchange, planning, financing, and the treatment of foreign capital. The broad purpose is to ensure a genuine common market, where the autonomous policies of members reinforce rather than vitiate industrial policy. Under this heading so far there has been some action to avoid double taxation

4

(Decision No. 40 of the Commission), and in other decisions there is an undercurrent of encouragement to 'state capitalism', so to speak, which may turn out to be effective, for good or ill, in cooperation. State agencies can go out of their way to be integrationist in their contracts; equally, they may be readier than the private sector to disregard the monetary incentives of integration, such as tariff preferences. But by far the most important acts of cooperation to date have been the creation of the Andean Development Corporation and the adoption of Decision No. 24, the common policy on foreign capital. Each has distinct over-tones in industrial policy. The latter is discussed in the second paper in this volume.

The Andean Development Corporation (Corporación Andina de Fomento), created in 1968, began business in Caracas in June 1970. It still operates on a relatively small scale, but is chartered to provide a broad range of financial services to the Pact, especially in the industrial field. It is entitled to raise funds in various ways, within and outside the group; it can underwrite projects, subscribe to issues, enter into joint ventures with local or foreign capital, provide revolving funds, and so on. The Corporation is especially directed to afford exceptional treatment to Bolivia and Ecuador, to support the activation of SPID, and to be on the look-out for ventures that are multinational in the sub-regional sense. Because its participations count as Andean capital for the purposes of Decision No. 24, the Corporation can in effect serve as an intermediary between foreign capital and local industry, public or private. It is in short a remarkably versatile instrument.

It is noteworthy that the Andean Pact makes *no* provision for a central budget, nor for any direct transfers from one member to another, neither to balance out the benefits and costs of integration, nor for any other purpose. Thus, quite apart from the concessions to Bolivia and Ecuador, there is a presumption of *dirigisme* in its industrial policy. It is also noteworthy that so far there has been no coordination of exchange-rate policies, nor of the various other forms of export subsidy that have proved to be such an important industrial incentive in individual countries, notably Colombia.

i. Trade Liberalization within the Group

The Cartagena Agreement requires that, except for one category of products, all restrictions to sub-regional trade other than tariffs (*i.e.*, quotas and prohibitions) should be lifted by Chile, Colombia and Peru by the end of 1970, by Venezuela within four months of its accession, and by Bolivia and Ecuador whenever tariff cutting begins to apply to any product of theirs. The last three countries are allowed to replace existing restrictions by an equivalent, but no higher, tariff whenever tariff cutting is due to begin for them, whereas for the first three the tariffs on restricted items existing at the end of 1970 could not be raised, and began to be lowered as follows. The exceptional category of products refers to those destined for SPID, whose restrictions would also be lifted only when the corresponding tariffs begin to be cut.

The rest of the liberalization programme concerns the elimination of tariffs on group trade. The schedules have required the adoption of a common tariff nomenclature, *Nabandina*, which is derived from the Brussels nomenclature via *Nabalalc*, the nomenclature adopted in the Lafta. It contains some 6,000 4-digit positions. An incidental effect, and another advantage perhaps, of the form that liberalization takes is that all tariffs must be expressed *ad valorem*. The liberalization programme divides products into two broad categories: those for which tariff reductions are predetermined (in the Cartagena Agreement) and automatic from a certain date; and those for which tariff reductions are *ad hoc*. In either case, once it has been made, a tariff cut is irrevocable. The *ad hoc* cases may not entail linear reductions — as, after an initial alignment, the general cases do — and their beginning may be more or less distant in the future. But there are no products, in either category, for which the tariffs on group trade will not some day be eliminated; that is, any exceptions to sub-regional liberalization are transitory.

The *ad hoc* cases are of two types:

1. Some 2,000 positions of the nomenclature have been reserved for SPID; in terms of tariffs this means that, for an interval of some eight years after the approval of a particular SPID, the member (or members) that may have been granted any exclusive rights of manufacture are to enjoy a margin of protection for that product against other members of the group; these others are required to eliminate their sub-regional tariffs on the product at once. The margin of preference, which is determined in each SPID, disappears before eight years if production is not forthcoming from the assignee; but the protective interval is five years longer for production assigned to Bolivia or Ecuador. Assuming that all SPID have been approved by 1976, the stipulated deadline, such margins of preference would exist until the end of 1982 (or 1987) except in the unlikely case that no production of any sort had begun. Only one SPID has been approved so far, for a range of engineering products; it is further discussed below. Reserved products for which a SPID does not come off revert to the predetermined and automatic programme of liberalization.
2. Each member was given the right to exempt from the liberalization programme a number of products for some time. Clearly they would fasten on those existing industries which, whether well-established or only just off the drawing board, might most fear competition; textiles were a widespread choice. These exemptions were of critical importance to the success of the Andean negotiations, especially as they related to the accession of Peru, and later Venezuela. Essentially, the four more advanced members are each allowed to exempt 250 positions of the nomenclature until the end of 1985, while Bolivia and Ecuador are each allowed the equivalent of 600 positions until the end of 1990. These deadlines will be extended only for very good reasons. In addition Peru and Venezuela are allowed further exemptions until the end of 1979, approximately 200 each.[1] It is intended that exports

from Bolivia and Ecuador should not be inhibited by the protection that other members will continue to apply to each other on this score. And in any case members cannot exempt from liberalization any products included in the first instalment of the Common Schedule of the Lafta (see below).

It is of course in the nature of nomenclatures that the number of positions allowed as exemptions implies very little about the value of trade or production involved. One item may be worth one hundred others.

Turning to the general, predetermined and automatic programme to dismantle sub-regional tariffs, three categories of products are found:

3. The products of sub-regional provenance that are included in the first instalment of the Common Schedule of the Lafta (Article 4 of the Treaty of Montevideo), 175 positions in all, have been entirely relieved of tariffs by Chile, Colombia and Peru from 14th April 1970, well ahead of the Lafta requirement. Venezuela is due to follow suit within four months of its accession.[2] Bolivia and Ecuador need not do so, though they benefit from the others' eliminations, until the end of 1973, when the Lafta requirement falls due. The products in this category are not negligible; they accounted for 25 per cent of the Lafta's internal trade in the early 1960s. It is likely, though, that in specifically Andean trade they are less important.

4. With one set of exceptions, products which according to a preliminary census were not manufactured in the Andean group, nor close to manufacture, at the inception of the Pact, and which have not been reserved for SPID, were entirely relieved of tariffs by all members on 28th February 1971. The exceptions concern Bolivia and Ecuador, which have been assigned exclusive rights of manufacture for 73 of these positions (Bolivia 34, Ecuador 39); in these cases the other members should cut tariffs only vis à vis the beneficiaries.

5. All remaining products (some 3,500 positions of the nomenclature) are subject to a most important linear process of tariff elimination within the group. Again, however, the process differs for Bolivia and Ecuador. At the end of 1970 Chile, Colombia and Peru all aligned their sub-regional tariffs for each of these products, either to the lowest national level in use or to 100 per cent (whichever was the lower); in some cases the reduction implied in this first step was very substantial; thereafter, beginning at the end of 1971, the tariffs applicable to each other have been and will continue to be cut by instalments of 10 per cent a year, vanishing at the end of 1980. The tariffs applied by the three against Bolivia and Ecuador in this category have been reduced more rapidly: a few were eliminated at the end of 1970 (on 63 positions of interest to Bolivia, and 51 of interest to Ecuador), and for the rest they will have been reduced in three annual instalments of 40, 30, and 30 per cent each, vanishing at the end of 1973.[3] Within four months of its accession, Venezuela is to dovetail into this programme in a straightforward way, aligning itself with the levels reached by Chile, Colombia and Peru for liberalization among themselves and vis à vis the two backward members. Finally, liberalization by these two (in this category of products) is to begin at the end of 1976, vis à vis each other and the other four members; without a preliminary alignment to a common denominator, it will proceed by 10 per cent instalments until the end of 1985.

The programme reviewed in this section calls for several observations. In principle, much of the freedom imparted to group trade is automatic and irrevocable. If they absolutely must, as when individual industries are threatened with dire disruption, members may invoke safeguard clauses in the course of liberalization, but only temporarily, with approval, and in any case neither for products in the first instalment of the Common Schedule of the Lafta nor for those reserved for SPID. By the end of 1973 trade within the group will — at least nominally — be entirely free in several categories, and tariff-cutting will be well advanced in others; products reserved for SPID are likely to be a notable exception, as will be seen. The evidence is strong that the notion of sub-regional preference and free trade commands acceptance. But the evidence is not unequivocal, and in practice several procedures can still serve to subvert the purposes of the programme: government purchases, state trading, customs clearance requirements, import documentation and identification of origin. Indeed, there have been complaints to this effect.

The programme is of course complementary to other provisions of the Andean Pact, most notably the rulings of Decision No. 24. Foreign manufacturers who do not intend to change into mixed or national companies, nor become multinational in the Andean sense of Decision No. 46,* are denied access to the liberalized market for their wares.

ii. The External Tariff

The general principle that determines the move towards common external tariffs for the Andean group is in the logic of a common market; members' protection against third countries should merge towards common rates *pari passu* with the liberalization of trade among the members, so that a common external tariff is established for each product just as all its sub-regional tariffs have been eliminated. If at that point, or even earlier, the external tariffs applied by different members remained disparate, the incentives of the common market might be distorted. In the Andean Pact this general principle is modified only in the case of products as yet nowhere manufactured in the group; members need apply a common rate only when production is on stream in one of them. Otherwise, as might be expected from the preceding section, common external tariffs are due to be in place for most products by the end of 1980 in Chile, Colombia, Peru and Venezuela, and five years later in Bolivia and Ecuador.

The merger towards common external rates is a two-step affair. First, mostly at the end of 1970, a set of minimum external tariffs was agreed for the whole of the nomenclature, except those positions reserved for SPID, which are subject to different rulings. These minimum

---

* See pages 23-24.

rates range from zero to 90 per cent *ad valorem*; as a rule, the more advanced the manufacture, the higher the rate. For some products, namely those in the first instalment of the Common Schedule of the Lafta and those as yet nowhere produced in the group, these minimum rates began to apply at once as common external rates; they are still subject to revision in the second step, but there is a presumption that they will remain where they have been set.[4] For the other products the minimum rates are applicable only if the corresponding national rate is lower; in that case the national rate must be raised to the minimum in five equal annual stages, beginning at the end of 1971. When this process is completed, at the end of 1975, the second step is to be taken. By the end of 1975 the Commission is due to have approved a set of common external tariffs (no longer minima), and the four more advanced countries are then given five years to align themselves with these, in equal instalments beginning at the end of 1976. Bolivia and Ecuador are given ten years to do the same, so that barring any special dispensations, which might reluctantly be granted, they should have merged into the common external tariff by the end of 1985, instead of 1980.[5] Whereas the first step could only imply increases in external tariffs (except in the case of the first instalment of the Common Schedule of Lafta and 'new' products) the second step could, at least in principle, imply reductions. The issue is discussed below.

The rulings that are to be applied to products reserved for SPID may be deduced from the first such programme, for a range of engineering products (Decision No. 57). As individual programmes are approved for each industrial class, external tariffs will be stipulated for each of the products in question. Initially these rates will require action only from members whose corresponding tariffs are below the norm; in this case full alignment is due as soon as output is on stream. Members whose tariffs are above the norm need take action only at the end of 1976; then all (including in this instance Bolivia and Ecuador) are required to align their tariffs to the norm in five equal annual instalments, which will be complete at the end of 1980. In the programme for engineering products, rates ranging from 35 to 80 per cent *ad valorem* have been set as norms. Interestingly enough, the programme stipulates that these rates are to be progressively reduced to promote efficiency, but it does not say when or by how much.

The provisions for a common external tariff raise some questions on matters of detail. It is, for instance, not clear what will happen if tariffs are cut among the Lafta membership at large (as in the first instalment due at the end of 1973): will the Andean group be bound *vis à vis* third countries by the tariffs applicable to other Lafta members, or will there be a split-level arrangement? Again, there is in the Pact no reference to the dismantling of quantitative restrictions against third countries, although their maintenance may result in disparate effective rates of external protection; every quantitative restriction generates an equivalent tariff, which grows with the suppression of demand for the product in question. And there appear to be no provisions applicable to the products which, member by member, are exempt from sub-regional liberalization until 1985 or 1990. Admittedly, in these cases the need for a common external tariff is still remote in the future.

The chief question is, of course, how protective the common external tariff will turn out to be; in other words, how much of a margin Andean manufacturers are to enjoy over foreign competition. The answer will evidently be of great consequence: it affects the efficiency of manufacturing within the group, it may upset the balance between manufacturing and other sectors — just as agriculture is claimed to have been hurt by the excessive protection afforded to industry in the average South American country — and it may determine the extent to which foreign companies are drawn into the 'revolving fund' of foreign capital invested in the group under Decision No. 24 (alternatively, it might put pressure on parts of the decision itself). So far there are few indications of what the answer might be, although it is clear, in any event, that common rates will not be simple averages of national schedules; these are so disparate that no average would of itself be reasonable.

The first step towards a common external tariff has entailed nothing but increases in nominal rates, to the agreed minima, and thus must mean, if anything, some higher protection, at least for the time being.[6] As for the second step, what is clear is that for any one member there are likely to be big adjustments in protective margins against third countries, for even after alignment to the minima rates remain widely dispersed. Beyond this, the general drift of protection is open to conjecture. Piecing the evidence together it can be surmised that the tariff will turn out to be quite protective into the later 1980s, but with a twist towards relatively more protection for intermediate products and capital goods, and relatively less for finished light manufactures. At any rate, such a twist is in the logic of the emphasis on 'basic' sectors. To promote efficiency the Andean Pact, especially in Decision No. 57 (the first SPID), does contemplate future reductions in the tariff, but at dates unspecified. And the special dispensation given to Bolivia and Ecuador is some indication of purpose in this respect.

iii. Exceptional treatment of Bolivia and Ecuador

A general principle of industrial advantage to the two backward members is indeed clear and consistent in the Andean Pact. It may be worth recording eight instances here:

1. The Andean Development Corporation is specifically directed to promote this purpose in its operations.
2. The design of SPID, and other instances of joint industrial development, is intended to favour Bolivia and Ecuador in the allocation of rights to manufacture; but, granted this advantage, they do not of course benefit from any further special treatment with regard to trade liberalization in these products, or the applicable external tariff. See 5. to 8. below.

10

3. Aside from the preceding, 73 positions of the nomenclature have already been reserved for exclusive production in the two countries (34 in Bolivia, 39 in Ecuador); they are products which were not yet manufactured anywhere in the group in 1970, and for which the other members are to liberalize imports from the two beneficiaries but not from each other; the reservation lapses if projects are not ready by 1975.
4. The two countries are allowed numerically more exemptions from the predetermined and automatic programme of sub-regional trade liberalization; they can hold on to these exemptions five years longer; and other members' exemptions should not be such as to deter exports from Bolivia and Ecuador.
5. Apart from the foregoing, the two countries start dismantling their sub-regional tariffs later: on the first instalment of the Common Schedule of the Lafta they follow the rest of the Lafta membership rather than the Andean group (and so eliminate tariffs at the end of 1973 instead of in April 1970); and on the bulk of other products they start only at the end of 1976 (instead of 1970). Moreover they can retain quantitative restrictions until these tariff cuts begin, and are allowed to replace restrictions by the equivalent tariff to start with.
6. In contrast, other members dismantle their tariffs against Bolivia and Ecuador quicker than against each other, in three years instead of ten.
7. Moreover the other members are to grant special margins of preference in 23 positions of interest to Bolivia and Ecuador, which means that in these few cases tariff-cutting among the others will be further delayed.
8. Parallel to their pattern of sub-regional liberalization, the two backward members are given five years longer than the others (until 1985) to dovetail into the common external tariff for the majority of manufactures.

It may be observed that, with the possible exception of 1. above, each of these advantages represents an invitation for the backward countries to take priority in production, rather than any direct transfer of resources from other members. Moreover the advantages are transitory; in most cases they will lapse by 1985 if not before. The view seems to be that the backward members should be favoured at the beginning of the course, but that by the 1980s all can be up to par; and thereafter, it is suggested, sub-regional growth will of itself be balanced, without transfers or further *dirigisme*. This is of course a version — quite static at that — of the well-known 'infant industry' argument.

iv. Joint industrial planning

It is one thing to free trade among a group of countries, coordinate their external tariffs, and let manufacturing settle or pack up where it will; it is another to plan the venture so that, at least for certain branches of industry, location is prescribed, markets are shared, competition is restrained, and complementation foreseen and encouraged. At its most encompassing this second approach amounts to something like the European Coal and Steel Community; but its simplest expression may be confined to two countries or one specific product. The second approach is of course still likely to involve free trade and common tariffs among the countries concerned, but under controlled conditions. It involves a preliminary assessment of the possibilities of production, an estimate of transport, raw material and labour costs, and a market survey, all at different locations and over the lifetimes of the projects under consideration. Without these preliminaries trade cannot begin to be freed, because planning would, when it came, face *faits accomplis* everywhere. The approach also means that national policies must be marshalled to support the undertaking; if a location is prescribed, for instance, the beneficiary must see to it that finance is available, that costs remain within the estimate, that relevant parts of the national plan are revised, and so on. All of this consumes much time and good will, and the imponderables are numerous, if only because techniques change, new countries are admitted, and natural resources are discovered. A group of countries embarked on integration would not wish to hold it all up until perfect coordination became possible, for that day might never come.

All the same, in the Andean Pact there is a strong tradition, going back to the 1950s, that joint industrial planning should be undertaken for the 'basic' sectors of industry. Here important economies of scale, location and specialization are expected once the base is extended to some critical size beyond one country. The list of basic industries has been invariable over the years; they are the heavier industries which were new to most South American countries in the early 1950s:

iron and steel	chemicals
metallurgy	petrochemicals
machine tools	electrical engineering
motor vehicles	
farm machinery	electronics
food processing	pulp and paper

Such industries are now to be found in members of the Andean Pact, and may even have acquired the status of chosen exemptions from the liberalization programme. Other members may be rushing to get a foot in the door before the joint planners close it. In these circumstances, a thorough-going version of joint planning would entail considerable rationalization of existing plant and scrapping of investment (with closures and bankruptcies); a milder form would accommodate itself as best it could to the *faits accomplis*. As time goes by this choice becomes, of course, unhappier still.

The arrangements of the Andean Pact comprise three forms of joint industrial planning, which fade into each other. In ascending order of thoroughness they are:

1. *Ad hoc* bilateral cooperation on specific products between entities, mostly private, in pairs of countries. The same enterprise may be involved in investment on both sides of a border, or one may have a long-term contract to supply another. These arrangements need not involve tariff cuts for the products concerned; often, though, the intervention of a state purchasing agency has this effect; in any case, the existence of the arrangement may be due to pending tariff negotiations, or is bound to influence them.

Arrangements of this nature, some approved by the Commission, include bi-national enterprises formed by Chile and Ecuador (fish products), Ecuador and Peru (drill-bits), and Bolivia and Peru (pharmaceuticals); Colombia and Ecuador plan to cooperate in this way on products assigned to the latter in the first SPID.

2. 'Complementarity agreements' reached under Resolution No. 99 (IV) of the Lafta, between two or more members of the Association. These agreements involve the elimination of trade barriers for the products covered, and the adoption of common policies on imports from third countries, including common tariffs; but in no case do they cover a whole industrial class. More often than not they are confined to specific products of interest to one or two companies operating on both sides of a border. The first complementarity agreement involving a future member of the Andean group (Chile) dates back to 1962; it covered five tariff positions pertaining to electronic calculators. At the end of 1972 members of the group were involved singly in three other equally limited agreements, in transistors (Chile), phonographs (Venezuela) and petrochemicals (Venezuela). More important, there are two agreements grouping more than one member of the Andean Pact, in chemicals (Chile, Colombia, Peru and Venezuela, together with Argentina, Brazil, Mexico and Uruguay); and another in petrochemicals (Chile, Colombia, Peru and Bolivia). All other complementarity agreements to date are confined to countries outside the Andean group. The last-mentioned petrochemical agreement is the subject of further comment below.

Complementarity agreements place the Andean Pact in an ambivalent relation to the Lafta. When the Lafta approved the principles of sub-regional integration in its Resolution No. 202, it stipulated that complementarity agreements among members of the new group should be open to other Lafta members as a matter of course, though they might choose not to join. A little later, doubtless to further its own more ambitious SPID, the Commission of the Andean Pact decided that its members should join new complementarity agreements only as a bloc (Decision No. 8). With the accession of Venezuela and reports of Argentine interest in the Pact, the matter may have taken a new turn. Chile, in particular, has been anxious to join the existing agreements on glass between Argentina and Mexico, and on pharmaceuticals between the same plus Brazil. How tightly knit the Andean group are to remain in this matter doubtless depends on the progress to be made in SPID.

3. 'Sectoral programmes of industrial development' (SPID) are a creature of the Andean Pact, in principle the most comprehensive form of joint planning contemplated, but so far confined to only one example. This is the first programme for engineering products (machine tools, or 'metalmechanics' as it is called) approved by Decision No. 57 on 17th August 1972. Judging by this decision, SPID are to be prepared as follows. At the end of 1970 a provisional list of positions reserved for SPID was approved, some 2,000 items long, drawn from the products of basic industrial activities mentioned above. Sector by sector and taking an overall view, a process of consultation and negotiation should then have begun, drawing together the secretariat of the Pact, member governments, and industrialists, to decide on the allocation of plant for each product of the industry in question, the margin of preference to be enjoyed by the beneficiaries of allocation, the common

13

external tariff, and other necessary regulations. The allocation would attempt to strike a balance between efficiency, as surmised from forecasts of various costs, and equity of distribution, including preferential treatment for Bolivia and Ecuador. The same product might be assigned to more than one country; and certain products might be found unsuitable for SPID after all, and returned instead to the general programme of liberalization.

It is stated in the Cartagena Agreement that the design of SPID should treat industries broadly enough to comprise in its calculations those products which this or that member may have chosen as its exemptions from the liberalization programme. The object is clearly to prevent these exemptions from staying out on a limb until 1985 or 1990.

Upon approval of a SPID by the Commission, the beneficiaries of allocations have two years (three in the case of Bolivia and Ecuador) to submit a detailed plan for the project, including its financing, and another three years thereafter to begin production. If either deadline is not met, the product in question reverts to the general programme of liberalization, where manufacture is open to all without reservation, except that Bolivia and Ecuador are given rights of first refusal on the products discarded by others.

The approval of a SPID by the Commission gives a country with an allocation of plant an immediate margin of preference, by requiring other members to eliminate at once all tariffs and restrictions on the beneficiary's product. After some eight years the beneficiary must also eliminate the tariff which the SPID allows it to impose or maintain. If a product is assigned to more than one country, these may either enter into a separate agreement on specialization, as under 1. above, or they must open up to each other's product in three years, by annual instalments of 40, 30, and 30 per cent (having first aligned to the lowest national tariff). Each SPID specifies common external tariffs, which act as a minimum until the end of 1976 and apply as soon as any output is on stream, and thereafter act as the target to be reached by the end of 1980. In this case Bolivia and Ecuador have to comply within the same time scale as the others. Strictly speaking, non-beneficiaries are not forbidden to engage in the manufacture in question, except where it would be in the hands of a foreign company; but they are enjoined not to do so for at least ten years from the date of SPID approval.

The first SPID, in engineering products, covers 72 positions of the nomenclature, whose output in the group is expected to reach some U.S.$300m. by 1980 (at 1970 prices, presumably international); 10 have been assigned to Bolivia, 22 to Chile, 23 to Colombia, 11 to Ecuador, and 25 to Peru; in 17 cases an allocation is shared with one or more members. Originally, 128 positions were to have been distributed, but 56 proved not to be negotiable and have reverted to the general programme of liberalization. Common external tariffs have been set, ranging from 35 to 80 per cent; in each case the same rate applies as the margin of protection which beneficiaries of allocations can maintain against other members for eight years, except when the allocations are multiple. Venezuela has not yet been integrated into this first SPID, but it has undertaken in the interim not to interfere with its smooth working — essentially, not to poach on others' allocations. If it were a matter of sticking to principles, its integration might be troublesome, for, by adding a new constellation of costs and resources, a new entry sets a question mark against a programme which, in principle, best fits a smaller base, differently 'endowed. In practice, however, even without Venezuela, the programme is likely to have resolved quite arbitrarily a number of imponderables, so that it may admit further manipulation without necessarily much harm to the overall efficiency of allocation.

In general, in the midst of continuously changing conditions, it is doubtful that the process of SPID preparation can fruitfully go very far beyond the obvious in detecting complementarities in production and avoiding duplication of capacities. Beyond the obvious lies a no-man's-land where what chiefly counts for allocation is a foothold, in the form of existing capacity, advanced plans, or a fortuitous discovery of resources. It is often difficult to judge whether the foothold reflects genuine advantages of location or an attempt to pre-empt allocation. It seems clear that the more drawn out the preparation (because of deficient information or resistance to any settlement), the less room is left for subsequent manoeuvre in planning. In this respect it is striking that the only SPID so far approved should cover only 72 positions out of a universe of some 2,000. And indeed it is a serious question whether all SPID can in any meaningful sense be ready by the deadline of the end of 1975. Events in petrochemicals aptly illustrate these difficulties.

Jointly to develop petrochemicals has been a keynote of Andean intentions since integration was first conceived, and yet to date the results are negative. It has not so far proved possible to follow up on the important, but limited, complementarity agreement of 1968 (Lafta No. 6), and as time goes by follow-up becomes increasingly difficult. The trouble has been a combination of new petroleum finds, especially in Ecuador, the possibility of new entries — Venezuela undecided until 1973, and now reports of Argentine interest — a general rush into individual projects by all members, and only fair-weather commitment to joint planning on the part of frequently-changing governments. Ecuador has still not joined Agreement No. 6, although the Commission has worked on the problem since 1970, and Venezuela is involved in another agreement, No. 16, with countries outside the group (Argentina, Brazil and Mexico); in any case the two agreements cover a different, though equally limited, range of products.

The petrochemical sector is one in which economies of scale are elusive, short of very large plants, and this accounts both for the rush into projects, for fear of being left out of any sensible group plan, and for its deplorable consequences as far as group planning is concerned. There is of course little chance that costly new investments will be rationalized away by a SPID, when it comes. Some of the projects in a rush are multinational; in one instance Peru has traded a benefit in the short term (low-cost resins from third countries) for one in the long term (manufacture of its own), by agreeing to purchases from Chile and Colombia while it installs capacity of its own in tandem with Bolivia; in this particular arrangement the other two countries have, of course, traded long- for short-term benefits; it is of interest, too, that a foreign company is prominent in the arrangement. In this way joint planning is increasingly pre-empted by *faits accomplis*, and the very dangers it seeks to avoid, the old problems of the 1950s and 1960s — excess overall capacity with deficient individual scale — draw nearer again[7].

Conclusion

Joint planning labours under conditions of imperfect knowledge, shortage of manpower, and margins of error which at times may cumulate rather than offset each other. Even without having to gaze into the future, it may not be possible to detect with confidence any but the most obvious cases of complementarity, to be encouraged, or duplication, to be avoided. With the best will it is therefore difficult to come up with unimpeachable plans to rationalize an industry across several borders; and then to know whether the admixture of considerations of equity (something for everybody) would or not seriously impair efficiency.

These difficulties preclude the rapid preparation of plans for all the main branches of industry together. All arrangements cannot therefore be simultaneously negotiated. But then, from one negotiation to the next, each putative plan is gradually overtaken by events: in part for 'exogenous' reasons, such as new countries joining the venture, new resources or techniques invented, costs changed; and in part 'endogenously' because, for good or ill, countries try to pre-empt the plan by installing capacity of their own. Indeed, with imperfect knowledge, existing capacity is bound to be a guide for the allocation of rights of manufacture. The Andean Pact is especially susceptible to these events, in its openness to new membership from the Lafta and its interest in planning basic industries — where resources and technique count for so much, and efficiency is likely to be found in a few large installations, too few to go around.

To expedite proceedings, the Andean Pact very sensibly built deadlines into the performance of individual industrial plans — two or three years to submit detailed plans, including finance, and three years to start production; but there is the danger that a reasonably efficient allocation, from a long-term point of view, may fail to meet the deadlines for business-cycle reasons: just then the country may be unable to borrow abroad, or strikes may have delayed the project, and so on. This is evidently an area where the Andean Development Corporation can be of considerable assistance once its operations take on a larger scale.

To compromise the search for efficiency with considerations of equity in the distribution of industrial plant brings further problems. As negotiations begin to stretch out for each branch of industry, the tendency sets in for national negotiators to insist on piecemeal equity in each branch, and for joint planners to surrender hostages to subsequent plans in other branches. Evidently, the existence of a central redistributive budget might help in this connexion — it is missing in the Andean

16

Pact; given a means of redistributing income, industrial plant might be more acceptably distributed on grounds of efficiency alone; and the higher income then redistributed for equity. Acceptance of a central budget is a sign of a general will to integrate; but if the will is strong enough, the other *dirigiste* ways will work without a central budget; each member will wait its turn, confident of an overall outcome to its advantage.

For the time being it seems that the strongest element of industrial policy in the Andean Pact is the liberalization of group trade, together with the indication that the external tariff will be quite protective — especially towards intermediate and capital goods. The risk cannot be excluded that the 'sectoral programmes of industrial development' are on the road to insufficient individual scale, duplication, and excess overall capacity; and, in the absence of a strong integrationist will to the contrary, the best hope may be that, when their time is up in 1975, these programmes will have proved so difficult to negotiate that the products concerned will revert to free trade within the group, with manufacture open to all under competitive conditions.

NOTES

[1] The Cartagena Agreement allowed Peru 450 exemptions until the end of 1974, 350 until the end of 1979, and thereafter 250 like Chile and Colombia. Their exemptions would indiscriminately protect any of these three countries against the other two, but not against Bolivia and Ecuador. Matters have been considerably complicated by the accession of Venezuela, largely because some of its 200 additional exemptions (until 1979) can be exercised only against other members singly, and then give rise to reciprocal exemptions which the other members can apply only against Venezuelan products.

It is also to be noted that the Cartagena Agreement sets out Bolivia's exemptions as 350 4-digit positions and 50 3-digit positions.

[2] Accession counts, not from signature (13th February 1973), but from submission of the ratifying instrument.

[3] As a minor exception to their mutual tariff reduction, it may be noted that Chile, Colombia, Peru, and now Venezuela, have left margins of preference to Bolivia and Ecuador on 23 positions of interest to these countries.

[4] For the products in the first instalment of the Common Schedule of the Lafta these rates began to apply on 14th April 1970, and for 'new' products they began to apply on 28th February 1971, or as soon as output is on stream. Rates in the former category range between 0 and 50 per cent.

[5] If the decision at the end of 1975 should imply different common rates for the products to which the minimum rates are already fully applicable in common (*i.e.*, the first instalment of the Common Schedule of the Lafta and 'new' products already on stream) the transition to these new rates will be equally 'linear, and will similarly distinguish Bolivia and Ecuador from the others.

[6] Only in freak cases would effective protection be reduced by this first step, since the less advanced the manufacture (and therefore the likelier it is to be an input into production) the lower the applicable minimum rate.

[7] The rush into individual projects may well find some justification in the present (1973) shortage of some petrochemical products, but there is no guarantee that the situation will continue until Andean output is on stream.

17

Investment in the Andean Group

AN EXAMINATION OF THE COMMON RULINGS
ON FOREIGN CAPITAL

David Huelin

E conomic integration in Latin America has been a talking point at
every conference and in every statement of economic policy in the
region for the past twenty years or more. It may be surprising that such
a well-studied subject as this should have been so little implemented,
and that the comparatively modest aims of the Lafta should have proved
so difficult of attainment, even after twelve years' efforts. The reasons
may be summed up in the simplified statement that, in matters of trade
and other aspects of national self-interest, the Latin Americans are ill-
disposed to make concessions to each other.

When the Agreement of Cartagena was signed, with the express
intention of creating a common market of Andean countries, few obser-
vers believed that it would be notably more successful than preceding
attempts. The signatory countries may be at less widely differing levels
of economic and industrial development than those constituting the
Lafta, but they are no nearer to each other in this respect than the members
of the Central American Common Market, and not noticeably more
friendly on certain issues.

The greater vigour and impact of the Cartagena Agreement may be
attributed both to the basic conception of sub-regional integration as
consisting of very much more than trade liberalization, and to the setting
up of an administrative Junta with a more ambitious mandate than was
ever given to the Secretariat of the Lafta.

Furthermore, by chance or by design, the members of the Cartagena
Junta are people of more impressive intellectual calibre than is to be
found, it seems, in the other administrative organizations. The Junta is
clearly ambitious to shape the development of the Andean Group countries
according to its own corporate philosophy, rather than attempting to

reconcile the divergent views of member governments by ineffectual recommendations; in this it is more akin to the EEC Commission than to any Latin American international body. The Junta has evolved a technique of issuing documents called *decisions*, conceived and written precisely in the style of all Latin American legislation. These decisions are not actually law anywhere in the sub-region until adopted by the Ministerial Commission and ratified in the individual member countries; but they are, so to say, pre-cooked and ready for instant assimilation into any country's body of statutes.

The Junta is fully aware of the key economic issues in Latin America today and evidently believes that their clarification, and the adoption throughout the region of common policies, are important factors in the achievement of real integration. The approach is an astute one; the difficulties of persuading originally five — now six — governments of differing philosophies to legislate in harmony are obviously almost insuperable, unless the hard work of thinking out the aims and mechanisms of policy is done before-hand and presented as an acceptable package.

One of these key issues in the economic development of the sub-region is the participation of foreign capital, where it is obviously desirable that no country should be markedly more attractive to the foreign investor than another, nor able to obtain development advantages over the others.

The role of foreign capital in Latin America is not only a key issue; it is also a burning one, on which there are more profound misunderstandings than on most other subjects. Decision No. 24, issued by the Junta in December 1970, and adopted by the Ministerial Commission on 30th June 1971, is entitled *Common rulings for the treatment of foreign capital and on trademarks, patents, licensing and royalties*. It has been amended, and the general principles have been enlarged, by various subsequent decisions, and no doubt more will follow.

Decision No. 24

Decision No. 24 appears to be the key to the political philosophy of the Junta, and, given the role of the Junta as policy-maker and economic coordinator, it seems likely that the general concepts of the Decision will prevail throughout the Andean Group, with or without minor modifications introduced to harmonize its rulings with national practice or sentiment in the individual countries.

Decision No. 24 is somewhat nationalistic in tone, and, because it is so formal in style and clearly intended to be assimilated into the legislation of the member countries, it was received in the developed world with some surprise and not a few openly hostile reactions. The Council of the Americas, for example, was especially vehement in condemning the Decision and telling the Junta that it could not work.

The Junta was not so naive as to think that Decision No. 24, simply by setting out the rules of the game, would of itself attract investors to the sub-region, even if its general adoption made future changes in the investment climate unlikely or impossible.   There is little point in having immutable rules of the game if the rules make it unlikely that investors would want to play.

What seemed to escape attention — initially at least — in the developed investing world was that Decision No. 24, though admittedly nationalist in tone, was by no means outrageously so; it introduced few new concepts and did little more than codify and rationalize divers existing Latin American opinions and practices on the regulation of foreign capital. However, opinion in the industrialized countries was taken by surprise, or even shocked, at finding virtually all known forms of Latin American nationalist sentiment concentrated into a single document and given hard legalistic outlines; furthermore, the prospect of the document's being adopted in five, and later six, countries seemed to represent an alarming acceleration of the spread of economic nationalism and a hardening of attitudes that many foreign investors had hoped might soften or even disappear.

Decision No. 24 appears to be, however, more a consequence of the spread of nationalism than an active cause.   It could indeed be argued that, by codifying the main principles involved in the regulation of foreign investments, the document may prevent or discourage excesses of nationalist sentiment in the future.

The main features of Decision No. 24 are well known; however, it may be useful to outline them briefly before discussing them.

1. Host countries reserve the right to exclude foreign investment in specific sectors of the economy, such as extractive industries, public services and socially sensitive activities; and also to exclude specific investments if they seem superfluous or undesirable.

2. Foreign capital should, as a general principle, be phased out over given periods, either completely or down to minority holdings.   Foreign companies that do not accept the phasing-out principle will not be eligible for the advantages available to national companies, and will be unable to engage in certain activities.

3. There shall be no take-overs of national firms by foreign interests, except in special circumstances such as the avoidance of bankruptcy; foreign investors may acquire an interest in national companies only when this represents an increase of capital, and provided it does not mean that they gain control.   Phase-out still applies.

4. Companies must have free access to foreign technology, capital equipment, raw materials and working capital, all at normal international cost; there may be no agreements binding companies to acquire their needs from specific sources or at inflated costs, and none limiting their right to export their products to any part of the world.

5. Foreign capital may be freely repatriated, and profits derived from it may be remitted within certain limits; reinvested profits count as new foreign capital and are subject, as such, to the regulations.

Reserved Sectors

Each of these points possibly deserves a brief comment.

1. There is nothing new or particularly surprising about Latin American host countries wishing to reserve certain sectors of the economy to national or even state enterprise. Mexico, for example, has legislated to this effect since the inter-war years and is still enforcing the principle of *Mexicanización*; and many other examples can be thought of, including of course Chilean copper.

There are three broadly definable areas where Latin American sentiment feels that foreign participation is undesirable because of the influence that foreign interests may exercise. In some contexts this is carried a stage further to exclude private capital altogether, presumably because of the possibility of an undetected infiltration of foreign interests or because it seems immoral for private enterprise to make a profit in such areas.

First, the exploitation of natural resources — that is to say, the extractive industries. It is felt, both strongly and widely, that the State should be able to control the manner in which the nation's unrenewable patrimony is converted into money. There are considerations of the pace at which resources are depleted, the extent to which extractive industries contribute to general economic growth, national control over prices, and the proportion of earnings that should accrue to the Treasury, all points of potential conflict.

Latin America's past experience of foreign-owned extractive operations has not been altogether happy, and it has long been felt that, where the product of such an industry is a predominant proportion of a country's exports, the government has little power to direct its own country's economic development. This of course reflects the fact that the foreign operator, being a large international corporation with world-wide markets, is free to contract prices, to accelerate or slow down investment and production, and in general to control the host country's export earnings, fiscal revenue and even to some extent its wages structure.

Second is the operation of public services. There is a general feeling, not only in Latin America, that public services are popular services and have great social significance. The operation of public services by foreign companies has had a vexed history, beset with conflicts over the desire of the companies to earn enough profit to maintain and improve the technical side of the service, as well as to remunerate their shareholders, versus governments' determination to keep charges as low as possible for social reasons.

The steady decapitalizing of foreign-owned public service undertakings in Latin America, and the deterioration of their services in the context of rising demand, is a familiar story and needs no repetition. Although Latin American governments that have nationalized, or rather 'statized', public services have, as it were, turned the old conflict into a domestic problem; the philosophical point remains that it is not acceptable that foreigners should earn profits at the immediate expense of the people, who have to use public services whether they will or not.

22

An extension of this principle now embraces financial services such as banking and insurance. These activities, it is argued, bring comparatively little capital into the host country, and there is virtually no transfer of technology. The Latin Americans are increasingly finding it objectionable that foreign banks should take the deposits of the people, lend them — perhaps to foreign firms — earn a profit by doing so, and remit the profit out of the country. The argument is perfectly understandable and, now that the Latin Americans are themselves competent bankers, it is hard to counter. Foreign banks do, of course, perform many other services, especially in the sphere of international finance for Latin American development; but it is not necessary to be a local deposit bank to provide international funds.

The third main area where foreign capital is not welcome — as already demonstrated in Mexico — is in the media of communication. Decision No. 24 reflects a common philosophy in excluding foreign participation from publishing and broadcasting. Mexico also excludes it from the making and distributing of cinema films. Here, obviously, the main consideration is not economic but political and social, and, one suspects, moral. Decision No. 24 also excludes foreign capital from the advertising and sales promotion business, possibly as an anti-inflationary measure, but more likely also for moral reasons. Whether this prohibition includes physical internal trading or only sales promotion depends on the interpretation of the word 'comercialización'.

Phase-out

2. To return to the five main points, the phase-out principle means that foreign companies should, over a specified number of years (15 for the larger countries and 20 for Bolivia and Ecuador), make their shares available to national investors. Companies are classified as 'foreign' if the foreign participation exceeds 49 per cent of the share capital; 'mixed' if the foreign shareholding is not above 49 per cent but exceeds 20 per cent; and 'national' if the foreign shareholding does not exceed 20 per cent.

These percentages may be higher, without a change of category, if the national shareholding is in the hands of the State and the affairs of the company are effectively under State control.

There is another classification introduced by Decision No. 46 of December 1971, which is the 'multinational' — meaning really sub-regional — company. Here 'multinational' has a special meaning and refers to companies in which nationals of more than one Andean Group country have a shareholding. Foreign participation in multinational companies is examined below.

The aims of Decision No. 24 are that foreign companies should convert themselves into mixed or national companies, and it appears that they could also become multinational. The incentives, if that is the right word, for this process, are that foreign companies will not have access to the local capital market, except for short-term borrowing, and will not be eligible for the benefits of trade liberalization within the sub-region; that is to say that their products will not qualify to enter other member-countries duty-free. This could place them at a disadvantage in relation to competitors that are mixed or national companies. These rulings do not apply to foreign companies who consistently export more than 80 per cent of their production; this would appear to refer mainly to the extractive industries, plantation agriculture, and fisheries.

The rulings of Decision No. 24 otherwise make it impossible for a company classified as foreign to market its goods within the Andean Common Market; a foreign company may sell its products within the country where it is established, and it is theoretically possible for it to have adverse effects on the competitive business of local firms in that country; but this seems unlikely to happen in practice since the authorities of any host country have the right to exclude foreign capital from sectors or activities in which it is not wanted.

It also seems obvious that, in industrial sectors other than the highly specialized, foreign investors are likely to be interested only when they have access to the whole Andean market; this they can obtain through the operations of mixed companies, in which foreign shareholdings may be up to 49 per cent, or through multinational companies in which foreign investors may own 40 per cent of the capital.

The multinational company as defined in Decision No. 46, which enlarges on the general concept of intra-regional investments enunciated in Decision No. 24, is one incorporated in the sub-region with capital originating in more than one member nation; each national shareholding must represent at least 15 per cent of the share capital of the company. Capital originating in one member-country invested under these terms in another member-country giving the company multinational status (the word must be used in its title), will be termed 'sub-regional' capital and will count as national capital in the host country. Investments from one member in another not complying with these rulings will count in the host country as foreign. Foreign investments from inside or outside the region may not exceed the stipulated 40 per cent of a multinational company's capital.

These general rulings of Decision No. 24, and also the concept of the multinational company, should be considered alongside the industrial programme of the sub-region, which is an apparently serious effort to promote industrial expansion on a planned regional basis, as Michael Kuczynski's paper shows. The Junta has thus, it seems, made the first attempt in Latin America to correlate the regulation of foreign capital, regional industrial programming, and trade liberalization.

These three ingredients of planned development are not to be found in the Lafta, which allows only for trade liberalization and industrial complementation — for what that is worth — but has no regulation of capital nor industrial programming at regional level. The Central American Common Market allows for the establishment of 'regional' industries in certain spheres, with theoretical access to the whole market, but it has no sophisticated regulation of foreign capital and does not appear to have exercised careful selection of the industries suitable for regional status. It seems, in fact, that the impact of foreign producers of consumer goods, using regional status, was extremely disrupting to local producers of the same goods, and may actually have contributed to the suspension of free trading in Central America.

The ruling in Decision No. 24 that denies to foreign companies the right to borrow at other than short term on the local capital market appears to be designed to ensure that such companies do not absorb local capital to the detriment of national companies; that they should be vehicles for the introduction of foreign capital (which is duly regulated); and that, if they need to turn to the local market for long-term funds, they should acquire them in the form of share capital, thus presumably converting themselves eventually into mixed or national companies.

In other words, the expansion of foreign companies — beyond that based on the reinvestment of profits — may be by means of fresh injections of foreign capital or by local capital participation, and in no other way. This meets the common complaint that foreign companies, by reason of their prestige, international connexions, or more sophisticated management, have some advantage in the local capital market over purely domestic or national companies.

Finally, on the subject of phasing-out in the sectors from which new foreign investment may be excluded — that is, basic industries, public services, financial services and communications media and publicity — Decision No. 24 calls for foreign companies now existing to become national if they wish to continue in business; in other words the mixed company is not admitted and foreign shareholdings may not exceed 20 per cent — unless the State is the chief national shareholder and exercises control.

Decision No. 24 here allows for the admission, in the first ten years, of foreign companies in the extractive industries, under concessions not exceeding twenty years; such foreign companies will be exempt from the major restrictions if they export 80 per cent of their production. In the hydrocarbons business preference will be given to service contracts between foreign companies and State agencies.

As regards banks, those that do not within three years record their intention of becoming national concerns by the stipulated stages must cease to receive local deposits of any kind. Foreign-owned commercial banks in the sub-region must thus change either their identity, nationality and ownership, or the nature of their business.

The other activities included in the reserved sectors appear to have no option and must be phased-out and converted to national status.

The group of articles setting out the regulations governing foreign capital in the reserved sectors contains an escape clause allowing individual member-countries to legislate differently on the subject if they wish. Although this clause was hailed with relief and even delight by some investors in those sectors, it would be unrealistic to assume that on this subject any present or future government of a member-state would think very differently from the Junta; there may be differences of timing in the relevant legislation, but in the long run it seems likely that the rulings of Decision No. 24 will prevail throughout the sub-region in one form or another.*

Take-overs

3. The third main point in Decision No. 24 specifically forbids take-overs of national companies by foreign investors. A take-over may be authorized if it is the only way of salvaging a company that would other-wise be bankrupt, with consequent closure and unemployment. If a take-over is authorized as an emergency solution, the foreign capital thus invested will be subject to the rules on phasing out, and all the other regulations; in other words, the taken-over company must in due course revert to national status.

Minority foreign shareholdings may be acquired in existing national or mixed companies, but all such investments must represent real increases in the capital of the companies. Moreover they must not be such as to alter the capital structure of companies — that is, to change their status, from national to mixed, or from mixed to foreign.

This ruling is clearly designed to prevent the process by which foreign investors have been buying their way into national companies, and often acquiring control. This has been going on for many years in Latin America and has given rise to much resentment, especially among purely national firms who felt the competitive effects of foreign influence exercised in this way. It can be argued that, even when a foreign investor acquires the shareholdings of nationals and thus gains control without contributing additional capital to a company, there is still an overall contribution to the economy, since the national capital thus released may be invested elsewhere; but Decision No. 24 does not recognize this point.

Technology and Loans

4. The fourth point, regarding transfers of technology and inter-company agreements between subsidiaries in the Andean sub-region and foreign parent concerns, seeks to ensure that such transfers shall take place at current normal cost and that there shall be no agreement requiring the recipient or subsidiary company to buy equipment or raw materials from specified sources; moreover the prices paid for such purchases must be normal, and will be controlled by the authorities of the recipient or host country.

* See postscript, page 32.

Furthermore, loans from parent to subsidiary must be at normal commercial interest rates and there must be no hidden charges; in other words, the cost of borrowing may not be inflated for the subsidiary.

Behind these now familiar notions lies the determination of the Andean architects to prevent devices whereby, under the guise of agreements on the development of processes, or other inter-company arrangements, the parents of subsidiaries in Latin America made excessive charges for patents, trade-marks, equipment, materials or loans. This has been done, in the past, to ensure that the subsidiary made no apparent profits, and that its real profitability could be invisibly transferred out of the host country, evading taxation and any limitations on remittances that might be in force. To the extent that the earnings thus transferred, without paying the tax in the host country, go to swell the taxable profits of the foreign parent, the tax revenue that should accrue to the host State is in fact transferred to the Treasury of the parent company's country, probably a rich industrial nation.

The rule stipulating that there may be no agreement limiting the right of any country in the sub-region to export its products to any part of the world is of course aimed at the not uncommon practice of the large international companies of dividing the world into markets, each to be catered for by one subsidiary. This may be a logical arrangement to avoid pointless competition between members of the same group, but its effect is often to leave Latin American subsidiaries with virtually no export market outside the region — a result that the Latin Americans quite reasonably resent.

There are some other stipulations in connexion with technology prohibiting any inter-company agreement denying an Andean company the right to adopt competing technology, or arrangements requiring the subsidiary to transfer technological developments of its own to the parent.

Repatriation of Capital

5. On the fifth point, the repatriation of capital, Decision No. 24 is quite specific. Foreign investments liquidated by the sale of shares to national investors may be freely remitted in the currency in which they originated, at the exchange rate of the day. Investments made liquid by the winding-up of a company may also be repatriated after payment of the appropriate tax on any capital gain that may have accrued.

On the remittance of profits Decision No. 24 states that this may be done, in the original currency of the investment, up to 14 per cent of the foreign capital employed. The ruling does not specify whether this is before or after tax, though since the term used is 'net profits', and since a before-tax profit of 14 per cent would attract few investors, it may probably be taken to mean 14 per cent net of tax.

Earnings above this limit may exceptionally be remitted but must otherwise be reinvested, when they count as new foreign capital.* It is to be supposed that in a mixed company, for instance, where the foreign capital participation was at or near its upper limit, the national interests would have to reinvest an equal proportion of their share of the earnings so as to avoid an increase in the foreign shareholding, which might change the status of the company from mixed to foreign.

The effect of this ruling would appear to be that the foreign shareholders of successful companies earning more than the remittable maximum will become more deeply involved, in absolute terms, unless they sell their shares to national investors.

It is not specifically stated that the reinvestment of unremittable earnings on foreign shareholdings shall be in the same company; it is to be supposed that they could be invested in another company, in the same or another member-country. This would provide, possibly, opportunities for manoeuvre and diversification, always within the regulations governing foreign capital. Another interpretation is that unremittable reinvested profits may lose the status of foreign capital and be classed as national capital, with no profit remittance allowed; but this is still uncertain.

The possibility of a foreign shareholder of a company established in one member-country investing in a company in another, especially if one or both companies are multinational — in the Andean sense — is interesting in the context of the Junta's plans for coordinating industrial development within the sub-region. Multinational companies are allowed by Decision No. 46 to participate in the reserved sectors specified in Decision No. 24. Since the foreign shareholding of a multinational company may be 40 per cent, this would appear to be a relaxation of the earlier restriction reserving these sectors for national companies, in which foreign shareholdings may not exceed 20 per cent.

All these points are likely to be clarified either in later decisions or in the detailed regulations that each country must issue once it has adopted any decision into its basic statutes.

There has been, of course, some speculation in the rest of the world on whether, and precisely how, the rulings of Decision No. 24 would be incorporated into each member-country's legislation, and how each country would implement them. It seems likely that, although the six countries may have adopted Decision No. 24 virtually verbatim, the subsequent interpretation through the *reglamentación* will doubtless vary from country to country in keeping with the current economic philsophy of each, with the need to harmonize or reconcile Decision No. 24 with existing legislation, and with many other considerations.

It is therefore impossible at this stage to form a precise idea of what Decision No. 24 will mean for a given foreign investor in a given country. To start with, two of the six countries are under representative congressional rule and four are not. Chile, for example, has already moved farther along the nationalist road than Colombia or Venezuela is likely

---

* Reinvestments of profits up to 5 per cent of capital may be made without authorization; above this limit authority must be obtained.

to do for some time; the possibility of changes of emphasis, if not of direction, in the policies of Peru, and the general unpredictability of Bolivia, are further uncertainties.*

Foreign Attitudes

It seems likely, however, given the none too felicitous history of these countries' relations with and experience of foreign investors in their territories, that the general precepts of Decision No. 24 will prevail, and that a desire to regulate the activity of foreign investors — not necessarily very restrictively — is now general.

This conclusion need not be depressing. A survey† conducted last year among United States corporations with interests in Latin America, to determine their views on the main causes of nationalism and how to counter it with appropriate safeguards, came to some conclusions that appear to show that the outcry against Decision No. 24 that came from the more vociferous sectors of United States opinion was not echoed by businessmen with long experience and extensive knowledge of Latin American affairs.

The survey showed that there was among these U.S. businessmen a keen awareness of Latin American hostility towards them, which they attributed largely to frustration and dissatisfaction with the slow rate of economic development, often encouraged by none-too-scrupulous politicians and then directed against the excessively 'visible' U.S. enterprises in the territory. U.S. business has thus been made the target of resentment, rather than — as one respondent put it — 'their own leaders who had failed to initiate meaningful reforms'.

The past conflicts and the so-called high profile of the large extractive industries and public services have been all too easily identifiable as manifestations of economic domination by foreign interests and a threat to the national patrimony. As Swansbrough remarks, 'the question of whether a corporate giant can truly blend into the environment is a serious question'.

The situation is further complicated by the undoubted hostility of Latin American businessmen, who fear the competition of the larger and more sophisticated United States firms; these businessmen often encourage attacks on foreign enterprise at the political level.

Interestingly enough, Swansbrough's respondents listed eight possible safeguards in the following order of effectiveness:

1. Close cooperation with host governments.
2. Firm rules of the game in host countries.
3. Local participation.

---

* See postscript, page 32.

† See Robert M. Swansbrough (University of California): *The American Investor's View of Latin American Economic Nationalism* in Inter-American Economics Affairs, Vol. XXVI, No. 3.

4. A hemisphere investment code.
5. An investment insurance agency.
6. Reduce investment in sensitive areas.
7. Increase foreign assistance.
8. Rigid enforcement of the Hickenlooper amendment.

The first three points and the sixth are virtually embodied in Decision No. 24; it may therefore be supposed that the Decision is not as repugnant to intelligent U.S. businessmen as it first seemed to be. The 'big stick' principle of the Hickenlooper Amendment and the dubious use of aid are both rated as ineffectual if not actually counter-productive.

There can be little doubt that Decision No. 24, though possibly inspired by the traditional hostility towards foreign investors, is not a hostile document and should not be seen as such.

Joint Ventures

There remain certain practical problems, not peculiar to Decision No. 24, but common to all joint ventures. These include the scarcity of local capital and hence the difficulty that foreign investors may have in disposing of their shareholdings to national private investors, as the regulations require. This could create situations in which, to ensure the fulfilment of the rulings on the phasing-out of foreign capital, the State — rather than private interests — might step in; it is implicit in the terms of Decision No. 24 that the State may acquire control of mixed companies with a smaller shareholding than that stipulated for private investors. In other words, foreign shareholders could find themselves with investments locked up in companies effectively controlled by the State.

A more attractive participant would be the Corporación Andina de Fomento, which could either acquire foreign shareholdings by direct investment or finance local investors' acquisitions, and might in any case be a more suitable partner for foreign capital than the State would be.

The reverse aspect of the same question is the inability of the Latin American private sector to build up companies of sufficient size and strength to compete against the large foreign 'transnational' corporations; competitive national companies cannot be set up in Latin America without the participation either of the State or of official international agencies such as the International Finance Corporation, the Inter-American Development Bank or the Corporación Andina de Fomento. Latin American businessmen are preoccupied over their own dwindling financial autonomy.

One hears many criticisms of Latin American economic policies, or lack of them, and indeed they have sometimes seemed rather misguided; this is obviously a consideration that foreign investors find important, but it does not detract from the validity of the attempts now being made by the Andean Group to coordinate and systematize what have hitherto been disparate and even unstable economic climates in the six countries.

It is obviously important not to look at Decision No. 24 in isolation, but to see it in relation to the industrial programme and the free trade plans, which in conjunction are clearly intended to avoid the pitfalls that have virtually brought the trade liberalization of the Lafta to a standstill.

It is currently impossible, without extensive market research, to establish the nature and volume of potential demand in the whole sub-region, but there can be little doubt that the combined market of the six countries must be worth considering. Investors who may contemplate joint ventures in the industrial sectors that have been allocated as sub-regional industries, with access to the whole market, should consider the possible advantages to be gained by establishing a competitive position early in the game.

It is to be supposed that once an industrial sector is considered by the authorities to be adequately catered for, further investments in that particular branch will not be accepted. This is not to suggest that there will be a furious scramble for privileged positions, but it does seem likely that, as industrial investors all over the world begin to understand the rules, the more promising opportunities will exercise some attraction and will be pre-empted by the more adventurous entrepreneurs.

Potential investors will doubtless have many reservations on the political future of a group of countries of such widely divergent philosophies, and indeed no one can pretend that they are all inspired by common doctrines. Their differences, and the zeal with which each government may be expected to defend what it regards as its sovereignty and national interests, may create obstacles to economic integration. Indeed, a pessimist might argue that there are virtually no antecedents in Latin America's history to justify the supposition that integration will be more successfully achieved under the Agreement of Cartagena than it has been under earlier pacts.

Even so, and allowing for the probability that each government will interpret the decisions of the Junta in its own way, there are particular features of the Cartagena Agreement system that seem to give it better chances of success than earlier attempts.

The Corporación Andina de Fomento*

The relevance of the Corporación Andina de Fomento to the question of foreign investments in the sub-region appears to be indirect but potentially important. Its role is to promote integration by the formation of multinational companies and to finance the inter-regional activities of national companies; it can mobilize savings, encourage capital formation, make direct investments in companies that it wishes to promote,

* See also Michael Kuczynski's paper.

underwrite share issues and give guarantees. It is the *instrumento de la intermediación financiera subregional,* but it avoids duplication of the activities of national development corporations in their purely national roles.

The CAF is empowered to borrow abroad, to negotiate transfers of technology, and generally to represent the sub-region's needs in relations with the rest of the world. It is implicit in the CAF's role, and its close relationship with the Cartagena Agreement, that its operations will be carried out in accordance with the Decisions of the Junta.

It is to be supposed that capital provided by the CAF will rank as sub-regional capital, even though it may be derived from foreign loans. Thus the role of the CAF as a sub-regional shareholder acquiring the participations of foreigners under the phasing-out programme could be important and would almost certainly be preferable to the intervention of the State. It may thus significantly diminish the danger, to foreign investors, of finding themselves locked up in a company over which they had lost control.

In short, the role of the CAF, if intelligently developed, could make the terms of Decisions Nos. 24 and 46 easier to live with than they seem to be at first sight. The activity of the CAF is not under the control of the Junta, but the identity of aims seems to suggest that the CAF may add some valuable cement-like ingredients to the edifice that the Junta is so carefully constructing.

Postscript

Since this paper was written events in Chile have raised the question of whether the new government will adhere to the principles of Decisions Nos. 24 and 46, or indeed to other sub-regional rulings. Doubts arising from reversals of political and economic philosophy in any country make it difficult for the Andean Group Junta or any member government to assert convincingly that in the treatment of foreign capital the rules of the game are immutable. Even so, it may be assumed that the regulations outlined by the Junta represent a code that is broadly acceptable throughout Latin America and will eventually prevail. This assumption is supported by the adoption of the Andean Group code, at least in principle, in Argentina and by the existence of concurring views in Brazil.

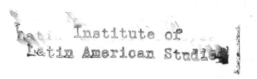